Contents

Acknowledgements

Many people have helped to make this report possible. At the National Children's Bureau a succession of individuals has built up a distinguished track record of work on parenting, especially Gillian Pugh, Erica De'Ath, and, most recently, Celia Smith whose survey directly preceded this research. Hetty Einzig, of the Parenting Education and Support Forum, has been a reliable and supportive friend to the project.

We are indebted to the Research Director, Ruth Sinclair, for her help while Christine McGuire was unavoidably occupied with her own parenting needs on maternity leave.

Kay Rufai and Stella Ilo worked hard to transcribe taped interviews, creating substantial files of data.

Outside the Bureau, of course, various groups have made a vital contribution. The Joseph Rowntree Foundation, ably represented by Susan Taylor, has provided generous funding to support the project. Its Advisory Group made many useful and well-informed suggestions: in addition to individuals already mentioned, thanks are therefore also due to Margaret O'Brien, Mel Parr, Jan Pearson and Sheila Wolfendale.

During the fieldwork a number of organisations and individuals gave enthusiastic support. In particular, the interviewees – men, women and children – were never dull and often delightful.

The experience of the research shows that parenting, and ways of supporting it, have perennial interest for almost everybody. Given such commitment, we hope that the findings will encourage further research and evaluation; if there are errors in this report, however, the responsibility is, of course, entirely ours.

Roger Grimshaw and Christine McGuire
April 1998

Evaluating Parenting Programmes

A study of stakeholders' views

Roger Grimshaw and Christine McGuire

SUPPORTED BY

JOSEPH
ROWNTREE
FOUNDATION

NATIONAL
CHILDREN'S
BUREAU

The National Children's Bureau (NCB) works to identify and promote the well-being and interests of all children and young people across every aspect of their lives.

It encourages professionals and policy makers to see the needs of the whole child and emphasises the importance of multidisciplinary, cross-agency partnerships. The NCB has adopted and works within the UN Convention on the Rights of the Child.

It collects and disseminates information about children and promotes good practice in children's services through research, policy and practice development, membership, publications, conferences, training and an extensive library and information service.

Several Councils and Fora are based at the NCB and contribute significantly to the breadth of its influence. It also works in partnership with Children in Scotland and Children in Wales and other voluntary organisations concerned for children and their families.

The **Joseph Rowntree Foundation** has supported this project as part of its programme of research and innovative development projects, which it hopes will be of value to policy makers and practitioners.

The views expressed in this book are those of the authors and not necessarily those of the National Children's Bureau or the Joseph Rowntree Foundation.

ISBN 1 900990 41 5

Published by National Children's Bureau Enterprises Ltd, 8 Wakley Street, London EC1V 7QE

National Children's Bureau Enterprises Ltd is the trading company for the National Children's Bureau (Registered Charity number 258825).

Typeset by LaserScript Ltd, Mitcham, Surrey CR4 4NA

Printed and bound in the United Kingdom by Redwood Books, Trowbridge BA14 8RN

1 Introduction

Parenting and parenting education emerged onto the political arena following the publication of a paper by the Labour opposition (Straw and Anderson, 1996). With the advent of a new government, they have gone sharply up the political and news agenda, making this study particularly timely.

This introduction to the research broaches some basic questions about the aims and outcomes of parenting programmes, many of which have remained problematic and elusive. It sets the scene for the research study which has sought to identify and compare the aims of the major stakeholders in the field, from programme funders and managers all the way over to parents, and indeed, children themselves.

Parenting programmes come in various shapes and sizes. In her survey Smith (1996) identified 38 different programmes, both large and small. Since then there is fresh evidence of expansion (Roker and Coleman, 1998). The proliferation of services makes it hard to be categorical about what qualifies as a parenting programme. But we would follow Smith in suggesting that a programme is a 'complex process of raising awareness about parenting by means of participating in a series of group sessions whose overt purpose is to allow parents to find ways of improving their parenting, or to feel affirmed in their own parenting methods' (Smith, 1996, p 2). It is not just about education, certainly not in a textbook sense, but about making parents feel both informed and supported. The term 'parent training' is a more specific form of education aimed at improving skills (Dembo, Sweitzer and Lauritzen, 1985).

This research has its focus on 'open access' programmes, defined by Pugh, De'Ath and Smith (1994) as being 'for any parent wishing to think about and discuss their own approach to bringing up children' (p 179). Closely linked to this is the idea of a provision for parents who want to do a 'good enough' job. Smith (1996) categorised together 14 programmes of this type, distinguishing them from 'problem-solving' programmes and those for parents with specialist needs (p 26). The challenge is to develop programmes that will deliver positive outcomes for a huge and varied population.

Outcomes

Over ten years ago, a comprehensive review of the field concluded that outcomes depended on the focus of the programme and the needs of different parent and child populations (Dembo, Sweitzer and Lauritzen, 1985). An analysis of the most carefully constructed studies identified positive outcomes for parents and children, but the type of outcome varied (Medway, 1989). Since then, some interesting studies have been conducted, for instance, in Australia (Allan, 1994; Barber, 1992). There has until recently been little systematic evidence about the outcomes of open access parenting provision in the United Kingdom and Ireland (Smith, 1996). Most of it is small scale (Pugh, 1994) or focused on one programme type (Davis and Hester, 1997; Parr, 1996). More systematic and substantial evidence relates to problem solving or specialist programmes (Barlow, 1997; Patterson, Chamberlain and Reid, 1982; Webster-Stratton, 1984). Nevertheless, there has been insufficient attention to the identification of desirable outcomes.

At the heart of debates about outcome are considerations about social function – what services do for society. Parenting education and support services can be expected to fulfil various social functions. First of all, we need to consider their **preventive** function. In this conception parenting programmes could help to prevent the appearance of problems in families and in children at some later point in their lives. Open access programmes are supposed to operate as **primary or first line** prevention (Utting, 1995; Sinclair, Hearn and Pugh, 1997; L'Abate, 1990). Obvious parallels are with childhood immunisations against disease, or social insurance.

Clearly, anybody interested in prevention on this scale has to look very carefully at what outcomes are desirable and, above all, at the priorities for prevention. For example, should the focus be on children's skills and ability to learn, on their safety and health, or on mental health benefits such as stress reduction, or increased social support? How far do programmes engage with the new social agenda of family life, caused by factors like the increase of lone and single parenting, the problems of combining work and care for children, and a rise in child poverty? If there are social changes and new priorities, we need to ask if there is in fact an agreement about the outcomes that people want to see. Parenting exhibits the diversity of society itself and any supportive measures will need to reflect that fact. Genuinely open access programmes would have to encompass the aims of the various social groups, communities and cultures in Britain today. So questions about aims and desirable outcomes must be answered before questions about effectiveness or efficiency are posed.

There are other functions that might be considered from a broad social policy perspective. One is the promotion of new standards of parenting. For example, some people might argue that children today should be self-confident or self-reliant (Hartley-Brewer, 1994). Or, more traditionally, it might be argued that they all should be taught a moral code. Such aims for parenting education involve **promotional** purposes. It is not solely a question of preventing harm or distress but of setting standards or disseminating values. Again there may be a wide range of views in society about what those standards and values should be. Indeed the promotional agenda is politically even more tricky than the preventive one because it raises broader questions about the diversity of values in society.

The purpose of the research is to ground our thinking about aims and outcomes much more clearly in the evidence of what people think, or more specifically, in the views of 'stakeholders' in parenting programmes (Guba and Lincoln, 1989). And among those, we include those who are organising programmes, those who facilitate them, those who refer people to parenting programmes, those parents who take part, those who know of a programme but in some way or for some reason decide not to take part; those who have not been offered the programme and have no realistic access to it; and the ultimate beneficiaries – children.

There is a strong case for looking at a very broad range of stakeholders' views because we know from various studies that the range of people attending programmes is quite restricted.

First of all, it is apparent that most people who attend programmes are mothers and it is not clear what role fathers might play (Dembo, Sweitzer and Lauritzen, 1985). Secondly, there is evidence to suggest that parent programmes are not reaching people from all social backgrounds. There are more middle class attenders than people from other backgrounds and working class recruits have been more likely to drop out (Medway, 1989; Davis and Hester, 1997; Parr, 1996). Another area for exploration is the participation of people from minority ethnic groups (Davis and Hester, 1997). So we have to think about the concept of **equal access** as well as the concept of open access.

Structure of the report

Following the **summary**, the next substantive chapter of this report outlines the study's **aims and research methods**, including the selection of programmes and the identification of respondents.

Chapter 4 explores the aims and objectives of those involved in funding or facilitating parenting programmes (the **agents**) in the context of local planning and delivery.

Chapters 5 and 6 explore the **parental perspective**. Chapter 5 gives context to the discussion by exploring parents' experiences of being a parent. Chapter 6 goes on to look at the experiences of those participating in programmes, and the views of parents (participants and non-participants) on the delivery of such interventions.

Chapter 7 looks at the views of the central but least visible stakeholders: **children**. Children's views about how a good parent responds to family situations are explored.

The penultimate chapter **compares the outcomes** envisaged by the various adult stakeholders interviewed and begins to draw together the evidence for the final chapter on a **shared framework** for assessing parent education and support.

2 Summary

Background, aims and methods

- This study focuses on those parenting programmes at the primary level of intervention, which are in principle open to all parents, rather than those which target parents with specific problems or difficulties. The aim was to step back from the question 'Are [open access] parenting programmes effective?', and instead explore what different stakeholders meant by 'effective', and how this might inform a framework for measuring outcome. A total of 80 qualitative interviews were undertaken with different stakeholders (commissioners, facilitators, parents and children) across three mainstream 'open access' programmes. Two programmes were mainly funded by health services, the other by education. Fifty-five interviews were completed with mothers and fathers. The great majority had children under ten years of age. In order to obtain a range of views, interviews were conducted with parents who had not participated in a programme, as well as with those who had.

Commissioners and facilitators (agents)

- The interview evidence suggested that the agencies and professionals involved were working to develop parenting education and support in a context where there is no clear social policy framework. Aims and objectives were formulated in terms of serving parents without reference to a coordinated plan. Managers and facilitators shared some aims and objectives but there were significant differences in that managers were more likely to identify strategic objectives such as community development or exploring new services.

- The context for the development of new services is strewn with obstacles. Genuinely universal services relating to parenting, in particular health visiting, stop quite early in a child's life. From that point, local agencies construct their own local agendas in providing services for parents, focusing on particular health or education outcomes; for example, parenting education as a means to achieving better educational outcomes for children. Although one programme was embedded in efforts to coordinate local agendas, it seems that collaboration on parenting issues is by no means universal.
- The range of parents that have access to parenting programmes is dependent upon the organiser's work role or recruitment strategy. For example, school-based programmes will recruit parents from their own school; health visitors target parents of children under five years, but recruitment can be dependent on patterns of contact that may mean needs are identified too late or not at all.

Parents (attenders and non-attenders)

- Four categories of parent were interviewed: parents who had been on a course and attended most of the sessions (attenders); those who had only attended a small number of sessions (drop-outs); those who knew of a course but had decided not to participate (refusers); and those who were effectively excluded from a course because of the way recruitment had taken place.
- A range of experiences in encountering stress, learning to be a parent and accessing help were encountered in the sample. There was little evidence to suggest that the experiences of those who had attended programmes were very different from the rest. When looking for advice, parents were keen to emphasise that they were discriminating in deciding which advice they took on board.
- Apart from parent-craft and antenatal classes, there was little awareness of parenting programmes. A large majority knew of nothing other than the one with which they may have been associated. These findings point to the very low public profile of parenting programmes.
- Over half the respondents (attenders and non-attenders) wished to go on a programme before a child reached the age of three years. Hence for many the option came too late.

- Motivational patterns among attenders were various, with some having a clear agenda and bent on changing their parenting practice, others open minded, or more interested in listening to other parents.

- People who attended sessions expressed mainly positive views about the group process. However the feelings of those who felt isolated and uncomfortable should not be overlooked. Such feelings influenced some to drop out.

- Parents strongly preferred a programme leader who was a parent or someone who was both a professional and a parent. The ability to communicate and to listen in a group setting was paramount.

- There was evidence of support among parents for the programme formats that they were aware of. Of those who had not attended a programme, many were happy to opt for the basic format described to them by the researcher.

- Practical obstacles to attendance were encountered by many in the sample, particularly the refusers. Parents regarded access to child care as a major prerequisite for their attendance.

- Most parents – both men and women – said they would wish their partners to accompany them. However, some wanted the chance to speak frankly without partners being present.

Children

- Children in the study were not asked directly about what they expected of parenting programmes. However it is clear that children at the primary stage of schooling do have an appreciation of the responsibilities of parenthood. They are also attuned to the variety of situations to which parents are expected to respond. They envisaged parents as arbiters, setting limits, and correcting disobedience.

- Children appear to be learning to be parents, as shown by the range of their responses to a set of hypothetical family incidents. Some of these responses correspond to the 'good enough parent' portrayed in parenting programmes, while a number do not. It is, however, fascinating to observe cases where tactics chosen by children do agree with 'expert' opinion. It is essential that children's views enter any debate on parenting education and support.

Outcomes

- Although the purpose of the study was not to evaluate the individual programmes, on the whole, the outcomes reported were perceived to be positive.
- Among the various stakeholders, there was a convergence of views about desirable outcomes of parenting programmes. Both parents and agents identified: positive outcomes arising from group support; a better relationship with the children; greater knowledge; and emotional benefits.
- Parents clearly emphasised group support and better relationships with their children. They looked for ideas from which they could select in preference to being told what to do.
- If parenting education and support is to be organised on a collaborative basis with parents, any framework for assessment must acknowledge the importance of:
  - allowing parents to share experiences;
  - inclusive approaches;
  - equality of access;
  - knowledge as empowerment;
  - children's views;
  - clear evidence-based policy;
  - strategic coherence from planning to practice level.

3   Aims, methods and sample

This chapter gives a description of the research aims and the methods used, outlining characteristics of the programmes selected and of the interview sample.

Aims and methodology

The aims of the study were threefold:

- To explore the views of a range of stakeholders on the anticipated outcomes of parenting programmes.
- To explore what stakeholders see as good practice in the delivery of parenting programmes.
- To develop a framework for programme assessment.

Stakeholders

Who are the stakeholders in parenting programmes? For the purposes of this study the framework presented by Guba and Lincoln (1989) is instructive:

- Agents – programme developers, funders, and facilitators.
- Beneficiaries – families who benefit from the intervention, and those involved in running, planning or funding the scheme, whose objectives are met.
- Victims – those excluded from the intervention, and participants or non-participants who perceived that they have experienced negative effects.

In some ways this classification is a dramatisation of stakeholder analysis, portraying those affected in 'good' or 'bad' terms. It points to a possible conclusion rather than guiding the investigation. One of the initial research problems was how to identify stakeholders who lie on the periphery of an intervention – the uninformed and overlooked as well as the formally excluded. In a sense children occupy a paradoxical position as key targets of programme intervention yet are often ignored as stakeholders with a potential voice. The research had to define a critical range of stakeholders, some of whom might otherwise be invisible.

The initial formulation was to distinguish attenders from three other groups: drop-outs; people who refused a place; and people who were excluded. In practice, refusers included people such as the partners of attenders who were unlikely to find it easy to attend. Among the excluded were people who had not been informed. These were not necessarily people who had been refused entry. As the findings will show, there are a great many uninformed parent stakeholders – far more than a marginal fringe.

Eliciting views

In this kind of investigation respondents must be free to express their views and experiences in their own words. For this reason, qualitative rather than quantitative methods were used. However, given the nature of the sampling method, they would not permit **quantitative generalisations** about the population as a whole. Sampling was purposive, that is, the sample was selected to offer a range of stakeholder views. The resulting pattern of data would then allow **analytical inferences** to be made about themes presented by the various interviews (Yin, 1989).

Sampling of relevant programmes

There were two stages in the research procedure: firstly, to construct a nationwide sample of parenting programmes, from which three were selected: secondly, to conduct interviews with about 25 stakeholders in each programme.

In order to establish a framework for sampling relevant programmes an announcement was placed in the *Parenting Forum Newsletter*, inviting programme organisers to contact us if they were running any programmes in the near future. A further announcement was made in the *Health Visitor*. As a result of these two notices, a sample of 48 options was obtained. A small supplementary group of contacts came through at a late stage.

The size of the response was excellent. But how representative of current programmes were these? It was important to ensure that the programmes represented in the contact list adequately represented the current range of 'open access' initiatives. A comparison was made between the data in Smith (1996) with the data on the contact sample. It showed that the most well known and well established programmes were represented by several contacts.

The next task was to select the programmes that best fitted the overall research objective. The selection criteria that were considered significant at this stage were, in descending order of priority:

1   *Range of parent stakeholders*
     Men and minority ethnic groups to be included if possible.
2   *Potentially wide relevance of the programme content*
     A clearly preventive, rather than problem solving, approach.
     Published and/or well known programmes (though not to be named in the report, so as to avoid the impression that they were being specifically evaluated).
3   *Funding sources*
     Single as well as joint sources.
4   *Range of geographical locations*
     Urban as well as rural areas.

It was felt that the programmes finally selected (see Figure 3.1 – P1, P2, P3) met the main selection criteria. Most importantly, they would give access to a good range of users and potential consumers in both town and country. In terms of content they were very much in the mainstream of current provision. And there were interesting features about the different agency environments, embracing health, education, and voluntary provision.

Interviews with adults

Agents

In each of the programmes it was possible to identify **agents**:

- particular commissioners and funders, such as a public health specialist for P1, the voluntary agency for P2 and the representative of the county forum for P3;

Figure 3.1   Programmes 1, 2 and 3

Programme 1 (P1)

A programme of seven sessions organised by a health visitor in part of a multiracial and multicultural borough of London. Parents were recruited by posters in clinics and by the recommendation of health visitors. The course was taught using a well known and very widely used set of published materials designed for parents of children up to seven years of age. Apart from a charge of £5.50 for the parent's handbook, costs were met by the local health care trust. The organiser's delivery of the course was assisted by parents who had already been through it. The course organiser had carried out her own evaluation.

Programme 2 (P2)

A course of eight sessions organised by a health visitor in a small town within a large county district in the South East. The course was meant to be accessible to a range of localities including rural areas within the district covered by the trust that employed the health visitor. The town itself adjoined a larger urban area and, according to the organiser, was perceived as an offshoot estate. Parents were recruited through leaflets and individual contacts made by health visitors. The organiser ran the sessions jointly with a parent educator who had been trained by a long established voluntary parenting organisation. Books and materials were made accessible on loan to attenders but there was no course handbook as such. In addition to £1 a week contribution from each parent, funding was provided by the health care trust and the health authority, by the local council and by a voluntary adult education organisation which had conducted its own evaluation. A crèche had been organised with the help of a nursery nurse.

Programme 3 (P3)

A course of five sessions, later extended to ten sessions, and run by a primary school in a South East town. The catchment area of the school included 'quality' private housing, council housing and social housing for the disadvantaged. In order to launch the course in her school the head teacher had sent out a letter of invitation to all parents. The course content was drawn from a recently published and highly detailed programme, which offered a range of materials including handouts for attenders. The head teacher had appointed an experienced trainer in child care who led the sessions. A county forum had been set up to coordinate the development of parenting initiatives. The adult education section of the county council assumed a leadership role, on behalf of this forum. It was offering support to the programme as well as evaluating the implementation of a variety of similar courses across the county.

- other managers such as the head teacher and the health visitor managers;
- the individual facilitators themselves;
- and influential local recruiters, such as health visitors for P1 and P2.

A breakdown of the sample is shown in Table 3.1.

After all the interviews were completed, a summary of the completed research was shared with a small and disparate group of health service commissioners and local parenting advisers from education and social services across England. While not affecting the substance of the research, their knowledge of topics such as parents' views or local funding arrangements has informed some of the conclusions of this report.

Parents

In sampling **parents**, the selection of attenders and drop-outs was comparatively straightforward. However, a number of factors had to be taken into account in drawing the samples of refusers and the excluded:

- the requirements of confidentiality in accessing lists of service users;
- the different methods of recruitment to the programmes;
- the availability of information about parents in particular categories, such as lone parents.

In order to contact a number of parents who were in touch with the agency providing the programme but had not attended it, lists of parents were sought from each agency. Parents were informed by the agency that the research was taking place and any with reservations were given an opportunity to withdraw their names.

In the case of the school it was clear that all parents had been invited to take part, creating a large category of 'refusers'. No one in effect had been excluded. In the case of the health trusts, recruitment was by advertisement and word of mouth, so making an obvious distinction between those who had in effect refused a place and those who for whatever reason had not been invited or knew nothing about the programme. So here there were both refusers and excluded parents.

Finally, systematic sampling methods were used to select a range of interviewees, including minority groups and single parents.

The parents were sent letters from the researcher. Where possible, parents' telephone numbers were also obtained and such contact was then far more productive. Attempts were made to insure against bias by targeting lone parents and minority ethnic groups.

A profile of the adult sample as a whole is given in Table 3.1, showing further particulars about the categories of parents interviewed.

The intention had been to obtain a mixture of categories in the sample. Of the 55 parents in the sample:

- 71 per cent were women.
- 78 per cent were white and the rest came from minority ethnic groups. The most highly represented minority group was African – six in all, including three war refugees. There were individuals from African-Caribbean, Indian, Bangladeshi and mixed backgrounds.
- The great majority had a partner, but nine per cent were parenting alone.
- Just over half (51 per cent) were couples (but were interviewed individually).
- Just over half (54 per cent) had been parents for up to four years.
- Two fifths (42 per cent) had been parents for five to ten years, while the remaining four per cent had been parenting for up to 15 years.

Table 3.1   Interviews with adults, by programme

	P1	P2	P3
Agents			
Funders; managers; facilitators; and recruiters (ie health visitors)	4	6	3
Parent attenders	7	7	7
Parent drop-outs	3	0	3
Parent refusers	8	3	6
Parents excluded	4	7	0
Total	26	23	19

All household incomes were represented in the sample.

- Weekly household incomes ranged from less than £100 to over £1,000.
- The largest group (18 per cent) had an income between £300 and £400 per week.
- Almost 50 per cent of the sample had an income below £400 per week.
- Almost a fifth (18 per cent) fell into the lowest income category – up to £200 per week.

As will be discussed in Chapter 5, attempts were made to assess the range of stressful parenting situations experienced by the sample. When the data were analysed, there was no clear evidence that the three programmes were dealing with a group of parents which had markedly different experiences. Nor was there evidence that non-attenders differed from those who had attended a programme.

Interviews with children

The sample consisted of seven boys and five girls, ranging in age from a twelve-year-old to one just approaching his fifth birthday. The remaining ten were from five to eight years old. All the children were white. Only one child from a minority ethnic group was old enough to take part in the study and, unfortunately, attempts to contact his family failed.

All the children's parents had been asked in previous interviews to describe *their* objectives as parents. All but two had parents who had attended one of the three parenting programmes. As there was no opportunity to meet these children beforehand, careful preparations had to be made, including a pilot exercise with other children of a similar age.

The initial challenge was to explain what the research was about, to inspire confidence in the children and to obtain their consent. It seemed advisable to focus these messages in a 'script' with mini-illustrations (Figure 3.2), which could be shared with children. The script made clear that children could pause, or halt the procedure altogether. One boy did choose to finish at a midpoint, despite his mother's encouragement.

It seemed sensible to begin with a 'warm up' discussion about the children's favourite television programmes (Ulich

Figure 3.2   Illustration from script for children

and Oberhuermer, 1993). The children were next asked to draw a picture of someone who was really 'super' at looking after children (Williams, Wetton and Moon, 1989; Collins, 1997). They were asked to explain features of their picture and then to help fill in parts of a story about a fictional family. The story took the child through a series of everyday scenes (see Appendix 'Child interview guide'). They were expected to take the part of a parent and to respond to problems and situations which had been constructed after a reading of the parent education literature (Tamivaara and Enright, 1986; O'Brien, Alldred and Jones, 1996).

> The quotations published in this book have been transcribed as faithfully as possible, but sometimes the punctuation has been left uncorrected to reflect the flow and pauses of natural speech.
>
> Each interviewee quoted has been given a reference code. For adults this will be a number and for children a combination of letters.

4   Agents – aims in context

A main objective of the study was to explore the aims of the people responsible for financing and setting up the programmes. In addition it was hoped that the research might give an insight into the way programmes operated in the local organisational environment.

Apart from listening to facilitators, interviews were undertaken with other agents who included: a public health specialist, community nurse managers and health visitors; a head teacher, and a senior educational manager with project responsibilities for several local programmes; a councillor, and a representative of a voluntary educational agency.

The first part of this discussion compares the service contexts in health and education; the second focuses on aims and objectives identified by agents.

The context for programme recruitment and delivery

From interview and other sources, it was possible to fit together a picture of how health and education services engage with and respond to parents' needs. What became clear is that the opportunities for providing parent education and support depend on structural and administrative factors which may hinder as well as help equitable local delivery of open access parenting education.

Health

Early contact with parents

Normally, health trusts contact parents earlier in their parenting, than do educational services. Group provision organised by health services includes antenatal and parent craft classes, and groups for first time mothers.

The comments of agents interviewed suggested that the educational components in many postnatal groups were ad hoc, the emphasis being on bringing mothers together for mutual support. As systematic parent education programmes, indeed, P1 and P2 were almost unique parts of the health service in their areas. However, there were obstacles to the development of further services involving groups, which are outlined below.

Workload management

The pressures of core child surveillance duties were cited as one reason for the low priority given to group work.

The critical time gap for prevention

Another obstacle was the gap between initial contacts, not long after the child is born, and subsequent contacts. After an initial period of health checks on the child, it was left to the parent to contact services if help was needed. For this reason, subsequent dealings with health visitors were not likely to present an early opportunity for first line preventive work.

Commissioning time-limited projects for meeting particular needs

Time-limited projects form a vehicle for meeting particular needs. In order to assist parents with difficulties, the district supporting P1 had organised a programme using nursery nurses as helpers. Promisingly there was multiagency support for the project. However, because it was time-limited, the project became a victim of general budget cuts. Only the intervention of the manager had restored it. She commented:

'there is no ring fencing of joint money that could be used to work between agencies.' (101)

Commissioning group work

Various problems associated with contracting were reported to militate against group work. First, some GP purchasers expected health visitors to focus on their own patients rather than set up a neighbourhood service such as a group. Secondly, as part of the contract arrangements, services were normally measured in terms of individual contacts. If these decreased as health visitors undertook more group work then the discrepancy had to be explained to the purchasers. Although purchasers were said to be sympathetic, this seems to be an administrative obstacle to the planning of group work.

Funding problems

If a programme was felt to need more resources than the health visitor's own limited time, sources of funding outside the Trust were sought. In the case of P2 the organiser did not have ringfenced time to run the programme. Given an apparent shortfall in resources from the Trust, she went to the Health Authority for help with printing leaflets and used her contacts with a voluntary agency to find money to employ a trained parent educator. She got support from the local council for a nursery nurse to run the crèche.

The pivotal role of individual organisers

Given these administrative obstacles, group provision was likely to be an individual's project fostered by a sympathetic manager who might have a vision but little practical room for manoeuvre. Commissioning agents made few influential contributions.

In both health agencies the format and substance of a programme were determined very largely by providers, usually the organisers, rather than by commissioning agents. The source programmes for P1 and P2 were introduced by their organisers and submitted for the approval of managers. In the latter case the programmes were also discussed with other funders. The voluntary educational body providing the facilitation formally approved the syllabus for P2. Significantly, very few new ideas were generated by these processes. P1 was approved by the manager with the exception of its religious appendices which were not to be discussed in the sessions. Evaluation was not necessarily performed independently: the organiser of P1 performed an evaluation herself. In the case of P2 an evaluation was undertaken by the voluntary agency providing the facilitator.

A series of obstacles to programme development was therefore identified in the health services. The individual agents associated with programmes were in effect obliged to circumvent them as far as possible. The evidence suggests that there is some way to go before programmes can be readily developed in a health services context.

Education

Increasing early partnership with parents

Even if health services are more likely than education to contact children at a young age, this distinction is decreasing. Schools are admitting children at younger ages than previously. Meanwhile, partnership with parents has become an ever growing theme of educational policy and practice (Malek, 1996). There are pressures for schools to establish this partnership as soon as possible. National Curriculum assessments begin early. There has been widespread concern about behaviour problems and exclusions in primary school. Investing in early preventive work looks likely to make good sense.

Parents' participation in the education of children currently takes several forms. One major objective is clear: parents are encouraged to promote the child's development and learning competences (CERI, 1997). The main focus has been on learning rather than on relationships or behaviour. Initiatives to help parents are therefore typically aimed at the child; any benefits for the parent are envisaged to be secondary. The provision of parenting programmes in schools is therefore a new departure, not only in practice but to some extent in principle. This certainly was the case for P3.

Initiatives from the centre

Compared with the health service programmes, the management of P3 was far more influenced by central initiatives. In the county where P3 was located, a multiagency forum was established. Adult education became the leading development agency funding new programmes in four schools. Existing mainstream provision concerning parenting was delivered in adult education centres. The parenting programmes based in schools were experimental and under the guidance of the central management. The source programme for P3 had been selected not by the school but by the county's project manager who also took responsibility for evaluation.

A school strategy

The head teacher is likely to influence strongly a school's partnership strategy. The head of the school that came to host P3 had made it known to the county forum that she wanted to provide greater support to parents and was offered the opportunity to run a programme for that reason. The head envisaged the programme as a means of establishing at the earliest stage a partnership with parents, supporting them by a structured programme that might correct mistakes and prevent problems in the future. This attitude was part and parcel of a caring, open door strategy at the school. Parents' needs were identified as a major focus of the programme.

> 'now there aren't the families around and they live perhaps without mothers and fathers near, who can give them support that perhaps in the village community perhaps 30–40 years ago they would have had; the sort of thing we are doing perhaps in that parenting group they would have done as part of a family setting and advice from parents, aunts and uncles, but now . . . they are very often alone. I brought up my children with no family around whatsoever and I know what it's like to have been on my own so I do feel for them.' (301)

In comparison with other local providers, this head teacher was particularly successful in recruiting parents to the programme.

Equalising partnership

It is possible to foresee pitfalls in the path to partnership. The county manager was aware that the relationship might become one-way, ignoring the parents' needs.

> 'I have a little concern about the word partnership, I am just wondering how much of a partnership there is here, and if again it is basically the school telling the parents what to do with their, to help their child, or with their child, then again as we just discussed, it could be perhaps handled differently, invite them, meet the parents first, to ultimately help them meet their child's needs.' (302)

The head teacher did a great deal to evade this pitfall. A deliberate attempt was made to avoid the impression that the school presumed to give lessons to parents. It was agreed that the school staff were not themselves to deliver the programme. Instead a facilitator with a child care training background was appointed. The head teacher attended sessions initially but then withdrew, feeling that she did not want to impose herself on the sharing of family experiences. In various ways therefore the delivery of P3 was distanced from the school. The role of the school was simply to invite parents to take part and to provide a setting.

The management of P3 was therefore innovative. The structure of an area forum linked to a centrally managed project with its own funds seemed a promising strategy for identifying and spreading good practice, certainly more coherent than the separate efforts of agencies. An equalising model of partnership was put into practice within the school. Innovative strategic direction of this kind contrasted with the limitations described in the health agencies.

Aims and objectives

The interview data was analysed with three possible types of aim in mind: aims relating to overriding social policy goals; local strategic aims; and impact on users. As it turned out, social policy goals were rarely mentioned.

Managers and facilitators shared some aims and objectives but there were significant differences. Managers were more likely than facilitators to identify **strategic** objectives for the programmes, such as community development or the examination of possible new services.

Facilitators were more likely than managers to mention aims that involved **effects on service recipients**. Two common strands here were a concern with *feelings*, especially increasing confidence, and a focus on gaining *support* from the group. Changing parenting approaches or solving problems were aims shared by some but not all the facilitators.

The relatively complex funding of health-based programmes introduced a diversity of perspectives on aims. The health-based programmes P1 and P2 were funded in somewhat different ways, P1 being reliant ultimately on purchasers and P2 having additional external funding.

Programme 1

There was some difference of opinion between agents for P1. A *public health specialist* of the commissioning agency for the trust emphasised the importance of focusing services on those who really needed them rather than simply offering services that would be swallowed up by the articulate minority. This caution was somewhat at odds with an open access philosophy and was not clearly reflected in the *health visitor manager's* thinking. According to this manager, Programme 1 was meant to develop networks of parents – 'a community development approach to get parents to talk about issues'.

Programme 2

From the perspective of its *health visitor manager*, the aim of Programme 2 was said to be the empowerment of mothers; it was not so clear whether there were further, more specific objectives down the line.

The two external funders of P2 were the local council and the voluntary educational agency employing one of the facilitators. Their aims were at different levels of generality. The *councillor* held a very broad perspective in terms of social policy. She saw the purpose of the programme as a way of preventing problems. The *representative of the voluntary agency* employing the parent educator – in effect, a provider – had a more specific goal. He focused on the effects upon the service users, in a similar way to the facilitators. Like them, the educational agency was more concerned with impact than with policy or strategy.

Instead of promoting change, P2 was seen by its facilitators as a way of achieving greater insight and growth, helping parents to be the best they can be. The greater focus of P2 on parents as people was implicit in one of the aims suggested by a facilitator: for parents to reflect on their own experiences of being parented. Interestingly the representative of the voluntary educational agency accepted this interest in feelings but mentioned promoting parents' communication with and understanding of children while the facilitators did not.

> *Programme 3*
>
> The *county education manager* said that Programme 3 was intended as an experiment to test out notions of good practice. The *head teacher* wanted to extend the school's partnership with parents – another strategic goal. She was one of the few interviewed to put forward a preventive objective: to prevent parents of children in her school from having problems in the future.

The fact that social policy aims were not a strong feature of the agents' responses should not be taken to be an oversight. Agents were aware of the larger context of parents' needs, describing ways in which they hoped to develop services to meet them. There was simply no clear frame of reference in which to set these praiseworthy aspirations.

Under the Children Act 1989 local agencies must prepare Children's Services Plans to meet the needs of children in their areas. In the plans for the different areas, parenting was given the greatest attention in the strategic planning of Area 1 (where 'good parenting' was the focus of a joint planning initiative) and of Area 3 (where parents in need of family support were felt to require a more coordinated service). However, it is clear that support for parenting in general was not a broad strategic objective, meriting little more than a page in the documents.

The absence of clear *social policy* goals reflects a national failure on the part of policy makers to create a definite framework for this type of programme to be undertaken. Similar queries can be raised about the *strategic* rationale of programmes. Strategic thinking about open access programmes seems to be relatively recent and the managers appeared to be ploughing fresh ground. For example, there was a significant difference of perspective between the representative of the commissioning agent and the trust manager for P1. Were the programmes to be about selecting users and focusing help or about building community networks?

The precise nature and extent of need for services among parents did not seem clear in agents' minds. Indeed, some agents felt that a survey would be useful in the future. Agents also felt that there was a case for consultations with existing programme users. Yet agents did not seem currently aware of any hard information that might entail a critical shift of policy towards parent education and support. Instead they relied on working knowledge and experience. An absence of research and evaluation created another obstacle to clear thinking, both in terms of policy and strategy. It seemed easier to think about the *operational* aims and objectives, in particular, influencing parents' feelings and encouraging group support – the most common themes across the three programmes.

5 Parents on parenting

This chapter gives the context within which the parents in the sample decided whether to participate in parenting programmes or indeed sought help from any other source on parenting. Such information helps us to understand what they may want from programmes.

The parenting role

Since parental responsibility is at the heart of current policy thinking, the views of parents about what parenting involves were of major interest. Key to their understanding of what parenting involves was the responsibility parents felt towards their children and their care. Mothers and fathers responded in similar ways

> 'All your time, all your energy and all your efforts, a lot of hard work. It involves a lot of responsibility. You got to try and be serious and think things out on how you would like your child to react and how you want the child to grow up. A lot of responsibility, I think.' (Mother 110)

Society and the state expect parents to maintain and support children in a material sense yet in fact only an eighth of respondents mentioned this subject. Issues of control, though high on the agenda of public policy, were mentioned by only a fifth. Again men and women gave similar responses.

Asked to discuss their aspirations for their children, parents nearly all envisaged them adjusting to society – having a sense of right and wrong, being happy and so on.

> 'Hopefully, they'll grow up to learn what's wrong, what's right, get their own families, get married have their own families one day, just be there for them basically.' (304)

About two thirds mentioned no particular goals concerning education or careers. Far from wanting to 'hot house' their children, the impression was of parents with conventional aspirations to normality and adjustment.

The stresses of parenting

At various points parenting is likely to become a stressful experience for the most well-resourced and adaptable parent. The interviews provided evidence of stresses, some predictable, others less so. Partly as an exercise to compare the various segments of the sample, a list of stressful parenting situations was constructed by the research team (Table 5.1).

A cumulative stress score was calculated for each parent based on evidence from the interviews.

- Over a quarter of the sample (27 per cent) were judged to have had no such stresses at all.
- Just a quarter (25 per cent) had been subject to one stress.
- Almost a fifth had been subject to two stresses.
- The remaining fifth had been subject to more than two stresses and the most stressed individual disclosed seven.

Table 5.1   Stresses for parents

Child
Three children aged 5 years or less
More than 3 children
Problem behaviour in at least one child giving concern
Health concern for at least one child
Disability of at least one child

Parent
Lone parent
Separated from a child
Young mother
Refugee
Depression or anger
Health problem
Housing problem
Concern about work or money
Partner unsupportive
Sees no more than one adult relative no more than once per month
Family support with children has been lacking or inappropriate
Household income less than £200 per week

Dealing with difficulties

When asked to describe the most difficult parts of being a parent, about a quarter spoke about lacking support. A large majority, however, mentioned the demands of looking after a child.

> 'The energy to keep up with them! Patience, I think patience is the number one key, being really patient with them and try and make allowances for the fact that they are learning every single day.' (107)

Asked to describe what skills they had had to learn, about two fifths mentioned patience, a similar proportion referred to knowledge, while a half referred to skills of caring. A variety of ways of finding information were described – talking with friends, family and services. Only a tenth of the respondents felt they had little success in finding the information they required.

Help and advice

Parents were asked about various sources of support. Over two fifths said that their biggest source of help was from family. The next largest – just less than a quarter – nominated their partner. The rest mentioned a combination of helpers. Only a handful cited help from friends or a service. There was some evidence that men were more frequently inclined to nominate their partners than vice versa; women more frequently spoke about help from family. Likewise the majority of attenders mentioned help from family. This evidence tends to suggest traditional patterns of support: family members supported mothers, while fathers looked to their partners for help.

Parents were asked to describe the advice they had received from services such as GPs, health visitors, nurses or teachers and to comment on its helpfulness. A significant minority, typically men, had not received any such advice. Contacts with services were more frequently the responsibility of women. In fact only two of the men made any comments on services. Almost half of those who had contact with services rated the advice helpful, the others were less impressed and just an eighth were negative. These findings can be compared with the results of a national study showing that four fifths of parents were satisfied with the help they had received

(Roberts and others, 1995). Most attenders found the advice helpful; this was not simply a disappointed group who, by attending a programme, were seeking, in effect, alternatives to normal services. Since they were recruited through mainstream service contacts, perhaps this is not surprising.

Besides services there are sources of advice in the mass media, particularly in parenting magazines and family-oriented TV programmes. Again a large proportion had not looked for advice from the media and those who had held a mixture of views, most showing qualified approval. Attenders were more likely than others to have found advice in the media but there was no difference in the proportion of men and women making comments, suggesting that both sexes are exposed to media messages.

A minority of the parents mentioned books they had used, like Penelope Leach's *Baby and Child Care* or Chris Green's *Toddler Taming* (Nicholas and Marden, 1997). Most of the parents who commented were positive in their opinions of the value of books. There was no clear indication that attenders were more or less likely than others to use books. Though a higher proportion of women than men commented on books, a quarter of all men interviewed said that books had been helpful or partly so.

What emerged quite strongly was the importance of personal judgement in handling advice.

> 'if something is bothering me, I ask their opinion (my own parents). If I don't agree with their opinion, I won't follow it through. If I do, then I will.' (106)

> 'Very rarely have I found people unwilling to give advice. In fact, you'll have more than enough people wanting to give you advice or "You shouldn't do this, or shouldn't do that. This is how you should do this." . . . But you've got to be able to sift out what makes sense to you and what seems right, what feels right to you.' (306)

*Parents filter the information made available to them, exercising judgements about what is appropriate to their children. They are suspicious of generalisations that are not tailored to a knowledge of particular children and their particular characteristics.

6 Parents on programmes: attenders and non-attenders

This chapter covers four main areas:

- First, the chapter examines the accessibility of programmes through the eyes of both attenders and non-attenders.
- Secondly, it explores the experiences of those who have participated in a parenting programme whether they completed a course (attenders) or not (drop-outs). This group of participants were asked what it felt like to be in a group and what they saw as the short-term outcomes.
- Next, the chapter indicates how far such a group-based intervention might appeal to those with no experience of programmes.
- Finally, it considers issues pertinent to future programme planning and facilitation among all parents.

Accessibility

In trying to understand the process of access, there were three topics for exploration:

- awareness of programmes
- motivation to attend
- obstacles to attendance.

Awareness

To clarify the public profile of programmes, parents interviewed were asked to identify any programmes for parents which they knew. Obviously, attenders, drop-outs and refusers knew about one course. A number of the sample mentioned parent-craft and antenatal classes. Apart from these, there was little awareness of parenting programmes.

A few were aware of a course that a friend might have attended or knew of postnatal groups. But 35 parents (amounting to 70 per cent of those who replied) knew of nothing else at all. These findings point to the very low public profile of parenting programmes.

Parents had very little background information with which to assess the relevance of programmes in general or to evaluate the information given out by people associated with a particular programme. The efforts of professionals to spread the word were vital: only one out of five people who decided to go on a course first heard about it through a friend or relative. This is understandable for the new programme P3 but also applies to the great majority of those who decided to go to the other two.

Motives

Three broad elements were identified in the motivational patterns of parent attenders.

A number of parents were consciously trying to **break the mould** of parenting set in their own childhoods.

> 'I couldn't see anything else probably because that was in my childhood too, I could see straight away from the first course that you do things that your parents do. So, I felt I was actually being too liberal with the smacks on my son, because as I said to you, my father was violent towards us, as far as I can remember and I feel that I was actually following a lot of his footsteps.' (105)

> 'they never take into consideration how the child is feeling, what the child is going through, they just become totally self-centred in their own way, the parents in my family, and my Dad was like that for a long time.' (107)

Others were more motivated by the wish to access **support from other parents**.

> 'Just to see really, if there was anything that I wasn't doing that I should be doing maybe and to hear other people, I think, it's good when there is more mums. Other people may have gone through things that you think, oh, I am on my own, I'm the only one that's ever had this problem. It's good to listen to other people and see if they've had the same things that you had.' (209)

A number approached the course in a spirit of **openness to ideas** which in the final analysis would be subject to the parent's individual judgement.

'anything that anybody can give you that's reasonable you should listen to it even if you decide not to take on board the advice, so I mean, then you have the choice. Once you have the choice then it's down to you, not anybody else, and I am very much in favour of, you have to make your own decisions, no matter how many people you ask about something, at the end of the day, it's your choice as to what you do.' (105)

Obstacles

Attenders were less likely than other groups in the sample to cite obstacles to their attendance. Two thirds of attenders could not cite any obstacles at all. Where obstacles did exist they were more likely to be related to feelings about the course than to practical difficulties. These were often revealing, showing, for example, how *stereotypes* about themselves or others caused anxiety.

'First of all, I am annoyed because I thought I want to go because I want to try and get some help and advice but on the other hand I didn't [want] to go because **I didn't [want] people to think I was a bad mother** . . . I get a lot of flak as it is because I am single parent, and people think everything when C fights at school, everything that goes wrong is always C, C is the son of a single parent.' (Emphasis added) (304)

Parents who had never met a facilitator were sometimes doubtful about the prospect of meeting 'pasta-eating Mother Earth' types or an 'airhead' social worker.

Practical issues were more salient for other groups. Two of the six drop-outs reported practical problems in their domestic arrangements that made it difficult to go, and a total of 12 out of 14 refusers mentioned practical difficulties such as the timing of programmes or lack of child care.

The prominence of practical obstacles should not lead us to overlook the influence of gender in determining who goes on a course. As we saw in looking at the data on contact with services, women are also likely to assume responsibility for accessing a programme. But the accounts of parents showed that practical issues were a major consideration in the eyes of both men and women. It is likely that, once practical obstacles have been overcome, parents' thoughts focus on the course itself and any deeper reservations surface in their minds.

The experience of attending programmes

This section considers evidence about the experience of attending a programme, particularly of group processes (Barber, 1992) and short-term outcomes (Dembo, Sweitzer and Lauritzen, 1985), whether positive or negative (Doherty and Ryder, 1980).

(Methodological note: In all but one case, interviews with people who attended at least one session took place within nine weeks of the programme's ending; the exception was unavoidably delayed for 13 weeks.)

The group process

Parent attenders and drop-outs were asked to describe the process of being in the group. Parents' observations emphasised how facilitators managed the group process by active listening.

> 'they just listened as well. I found that [one of the facilitators] did a lot but I think she's the parenting one. Had their views of what may have worked and things but [the other one] I assumed she listened. I often sort of looked round and she was sitting listening to everybody, I think.' (209)

It was perceived that facilitators used the group as an echo chamber, sounding out ideas from the programme curriculum.

> 'I think [the facilitator] felt that it's not so much what's in the book that really makes the difference in how things are actually put across, it's how the group as a whole interacts and understands and how much information can be put into it by all the participants, and how it all comes out in the wash basically, because, it's true, because you've seen what it's like. It goes in one way, it goes in saying, that's one particular one thing and then like it comes out and it might be exactly the same thing but you are thinking of it in a totally different way because of other people's views, and the way they would interpret what's been given to them.' (105)

The involvement of parents in facilitation was seen as adding credibility.

> 'They had Mums on there from previous ones which gave you confidence to say look someone's gone and now they are helping somebody else, ooh that must work. It gives you the idea, oh they are coming back, so it must be quite good.' (107)

The way in which ideas were communicated meant that messages were not set in stone and handed down.

'**if there was a message** it was that to pay more attention to your children, I suppose, because a lot of things they did, we discovered was because they wanted more attention. So right or wrong, they were doing naughty things to gain attention.' (Emphasis added) (308)

Outcomes were defined in emotional as much as educational terms. Asked to say what she had got out of the course one said:

'Quite a bit, I certainly feel more confident than I did and I don't lose my temper as much, I am a bit more tolerant.' (308)

It was possible to sum up the opinions of the parents who had attended sessions by comparing responses to five separate questions (Table 6.1).

Table 6.1   Ratings of process (25 cases)

Approach of facilitator valued
Ease in talking within the group
Understood a message from programme
Clarity of message
No doubts about continuing to the last session

Full satisfaction would have been represented by five positive replies; in fact, the median was 3.5. Attenders were significantly more likely than drop-outs to be positive about their experiences. There were no significant differences among parents involved with the three programmes.

For a number of parents, not necessarily drop-outs, the group process was problematic. These feelings are described in the next subsection.

A sense of isolation

Feeling isolated was a common experience among people who did not conform to the typical profile of attenders. The most obvious of these marginals was the sole male attender who was uncomfortable with the facilitator's approach.

'A lot of the angle that she was coming from and a lot of things that she was talking about were all from a female perspective.

Obviously she is a woman herself, but they were being aimed at a female audience, and she kept on saying, "Oh, and Dads", it was almost like "Oh sorry I forgot you were there".' (306)

For the young refugees the experience of the group gave them a similar sense of isolation as foreigners.

114:      'everything was fine except no other community.'
Roger: 'And you told me earlier, that you felt like a foreigner. Why did you feel like a foreigner?'
114:      'I felt, everybody knew each other, even if they did not, but I was shy, quiet and at the same time my English was not good.'

Being a working mother could feel odd when surrounded by homemakers with traditional views about the virtues of full time parenting.

'there was . . . a certain view which a lot of the other parents had about working mothers. I was the only mother who worked in the day, and I couldn't believe it. They actually said things about mothers not being there for the children and I found that very difficult.' (309)

A parent who wanted some serious advice felt excluded by the chit-chat.

'it just got to the point where there was the cliquey, like all the mothers that meet up for keep fit, sort of thing, it was like a night out, that was the impression, oh, it was nothing, it was a usage of, you know, to go out for the night.' (317)

Looking at the sample as a whole, this experience of feeling isolated extended beyond the man to include a number of individuals – a full time working mother, a single mother, and the refugees.

Dropping out

Two mothers dropped out having failed to attend the first session.

'I was going to go but like I said, I'd gone shopping in the morning and got stuck in the rain and I didn't have any rain gear for the pram, so I was late going, and I thought if I missed the first one then not go to the next one. Then he started to get better, so sleeping again and I didn't bother.' (117)

Another dropped out after two sessions for practical reasons.

'It's just unfortunate the evening it fell on because it was the evening that my husband had always gone out and one evening one of the boys was ill and I was just unable to go.' (107)

Feeling the whole course lacked substance discouraged one from continuing.

'Yeah, the whole time, [the facilitator talked] yep, yep, yep, about her experiences and although there was like a group discussion, it was about stupid little things, you know that you think, oh, you should know that, you are a mother. It was common sense things.' (317)

The refugees dropped out, finding the group discussion hard to follow.

A mixture of practical and other problems influenced the process of dropping out. For most the main remedy seemed to be one of strengthening their access to the programme rather than bringing in an alternative agenda of issues. For speaker 317, who wanted serious advice about behaviour problems, the level of discussion was too basic to encourage her participation. For all these parents the group process failed the test of inclusiveness.

Outcomes of the programmes

From process we now turn to outcome. Here is one example of a parent explaining the benefits of a course.

Roger: 'Looking back on all the sessions that you attended, how much did you get out of the course?'

211: 'It taught me to look at things from a different angle on some of them and there is a lot of the time when you are about to bawl and yell and lose your rag and you think, no, hang on a minute, count to 10, you know, readjust it, let's come at this from a different angle and that has helped. You don't always remember to do it but it certainly helps to defuse the situation a lot of the times.'

Based on replies to five questions (Table 6.2), the satisfaction of parents who had experience of the courses was measured. It was found that the median score was 4, out of a possible 5. Attenders were more appreciative about the outcomes than drop-outs. There were no differences among the ratings for the three programmes.

Table 6.2   Positive outcomes (25 cases)

Positive feelings at end of course
How much got out of course
Benefit to child
No drawbacks experienced
Ease in implementing programme messages

Interest in programmes among non-attenders

The low public profile of programmes meant that clear evidence about the attitudes of non-attenders could only be obtained by first presenting them with basic information about pro- grammes. After they had been given the information and the opportunity to ask questions, the level of interest which they expressed was relatively high (Table 6.3). A number would have wanted this service in the past but felt that it would not be appropriate now. Others would only want the service if they had a problem or they wanted more specific help. A few were more comfortable with a TV or video presentation.

Table 6.3   Interest in parenting programmes among non-attenders

	All (N=30)	Men
Yes	12	7
Possibly in the past	5	2
Only if I had a problem	6	1
No	2	1
Can't attend	2	2
Other kind of service	1	0
TV/Video	2	1

There was little evidence that parents feared some breach of confidentiality as a result of attending a group. Only four respondents mentioned this concern. A dozen could think of other possible disadvantages, such as doubt being instilled, loss of confidence, being dictated to or not getting on with the group. One who felt that there might be a stigma in going on a course said that a supportive network would help to combat such feelings.

Preferences about access and delivery

The best stage to attend

Parents who had attended sessions or expressed an interest in doing so were asked to say when they might prefer to take part (Table 6.4). These parents had been involved in parenting for up to 15 years.

Table 6.4   Best stage to attend, by gender (N=48)

Stage	Males	Females
Before pregnancy	2	1
Pregnancy	2	4
First year	0	11
2–3 years	2	4
At key points	3	6
If problem	1	3
No preference	2	2
5 years	0	2
6 years	0	1
Continuously	1	0
In past	1	0
Total	14	34

Over half the respondents wished to access a programme before a child reached the age of three years.

'I found out about them by accident but I wish I'd found out about it earlier, a lot earlier, and I think perhaps, it's something they should hand out after you've had a baby or something, or at the health clinic, when you go up to weigh in and the health visitors should point these things out.' (208)

The most popular option was to go on a programme in the child's first year but this idea occurred to none of the men. Even among the parents with school age children there was a clear preference for an earlier opportunity to attend. Such findings lead to the conclusion that **early access** aimed at parents of children under three years of age would best fit parental wishes.

Leadership

Parents were asked to say what kind of person should be 'a leader'. There was a strong preference for someone who was a parent, or who was both a professional and a parent (Table 6.5).

Table 6.5 Preferences about leader (N=43)

Parent	17
Professional and parent	15
Professional	6
Trained parent	1
Mixed or other preference	3

Asked to describe the qualities of a leader, nearly all respondents mentioned qualities associated with group counselling and facilitation, such as the ability to communicate and to listen, friendliness, patience, openness and compassion.

'The person has to be patient, has to be understanding, has to be able to express herself, like I said, she must have had some experiences to be able to get across to people and must make it very interesting, so it is not a boring long talk.' (125)

'[My model leader] is an active listener actually, I think, which is what I like, if I am talking to someone. And the other thing, is, she wants you to think for yourself, she doesn't want to give you the answers all the time.' (316)

Partners' participation

If parents are to work together to bring up children, then finding ways to harmonise their approaches is vital. Attitudes to the participation of partners were therefore explored (see Table 6.6).

Most parents – both men and women – said they would wish their partners to accompany them. However, some were certainly doubtful, feeling that the group discussion would not be so frank or allow feelings to be expressed.

Table 6.6   'Wish partner to attend with me'
– responses

Yes	29
Qualified Yes	6
No	5
Fathers-only course	2
Have options	1
Don't know	1
No response/missing	11
Total	55

'I mean [my husband] went to Parents Craft with me but I wouldn't say he learned anything. I think it's somewhere, where mums can let go and we can have a moan about the husbands. You can't really do that if they are there. I do remember warning you about this when you came to the room for the first meeting!' (208)

Fathers' programmes were not the first choice of many. As one put it:

'I just don't think it's in the male make-up to sit there and talk about, I suppose it's interesting for a little while but I don't think blokes tend to click so well.' (220)

Going together was felt to be an option confronted by obstacles, such as lack of child care.

'some people would need babysitters. Otherwise that would stop both of them coming.' (121)

Help to attend

When asked what help they might need, regardless of their preferences about attending with partners, a large majority mentioned child care as a basic prerequisite for attendance. For single parents, cost might be a major deterrent.

'the only thing that I do suffer from is babysitters, the young girl down the road costs me £5 each time I have a babysitter. I am not in a financial situation to keep paying out £5 here and there for a babysitter.' (304)

Only an eighth of respondents mentioned their work arrangements. A similar proportion mentioned either some combination of these or another kind of help.

The data show that child care is a fundamental factor to be taken into account in considering programme access. The form of any support or provision would be particularly crucial if parents wish to attend when children are young.

Content

The 51 parents with some interest or experience were asked what they wanted to be included in an ideal programme. Fourteen of those who had attended sessions opted for what they had experienced. Seven of the rest were happy to go along with what had been described to them. Further options were explored with the respondents as the interview continued.

About a quarter of the respondents expressed interest in family and social issues, in child behaviour and so on. A similar proportion wanted information about child development or health. Fewer – just one in ten – were interested in educational issues for their children. More personal topics and feelings were not raised. There were several other formulations or suggestions mentioned, such as targeting a small age group of children.

A single parent wanted a course specifically for single parents, thus confirming the importance of considering individual needs in a group setting.

Other comments tended to bring in considerations of outcome which were the subject of questions later in the interview.

7 Children on parenting

Children are the most important stakeholders in parenting education, yet critics allege that programmes treat them as objects rather than as partners (Hess, 1980; Doherty and Ryder, 1980). If children are to be acknowledged as stakeholders in their own right, then attention must focus on the conceptual learning process by which they become potential partners in parenting discussions (Selman, 1980).

The aims of the interviews with children were: to identify the extent to which children are learning to be parents; to explore how children perceive the responsibilities of parenthood; and to compare their tactics of communication with those recommended in the literature of parenting programmes.

Children fell willingly to the task of drawing, portraying parents in various guises: as partners in enjoyable experiences (playing games, or going to the zoo), as housekeepers and shoppers, or as stylish. One of the super Mums had hair bunches like Baby Spice! A boy was the only one to venture into the imaginary, depicting a ministering angel helping poor children. But the oldest, a twelve-year-old, declined to produce a drawing, reflecting a common drop in children's interest in this activity as they grow up.

While one or two of the group found parts of the story exercise a little difficult, it became very apparent that these children, mostly five to eight years old, had clear perceptions of how parents should respond to the normal demands and dilemmas of looking after children. The responses of the children are set out in the following subsections, in the order of the narrative.

Secure limits

Typically the children gave instructions or warnings to a child who might fall into danger playing near a road (Table 7.1).

Table 7.1   Responses

Instruction (forbidding)	5
Instruction (to accompany parent)	3
Warning	5

In the instructions, there were a mixture of messages, both 'positive' ('Do this') and 'negative' ('Don't do that'), (see Parent Network (1988) in References section, *Labels*, p 8).

CKM: 'I'd say No, because it's too dangerous.'

CJM: 'when the traffic's gone, you can go over there, but if the traffic comes back, just come back.'

Warnings without actual instructions were given by four older children, suggesting they placed greater reliance on children taking responsibility for their own safety.

The responses indicated that children expected parents to be protective; they used a mixture of ways of communicating that basic message.

Encouragement – play in the living room

Children's play has long been acknowledged as a developmental opportunity. Yet some influential programmes also advise parents to take a specific encouraging role – 'play-listening' (Quinn and Quinn, 1995).

A number of children interpreted the play scenario as the child's inappropriate use of living room space (Table 7.2). In their eyes, the bedroom was the proper place for playing with Lego. Others were prepared to help or make suggestions. None adopted the more passive standpoint of 'play-listening'. Two saw the scenario as an opportunity to give warnings on other matters, such as checking that the child had tidied up his or her own bedroom.

Table 7.2   Responses

Inappropriate place for play	5
Help or make suggestion	4
Warnings on other matters	2

Disobedience

Children were asked to imagine any situation in which the child did something forbidden and then repeated it a second time. The imaginary scenarios ranged from 'playing in the mud' and 'bouncing on the sofa' to 'smashing bottles in the roadway'.

None thought the misbehaviour should be ignored. One child labelled the offender as naughty, gave a punishment and then repeated it after further disobedience. Four of the children used a clear escalation technique, involving an instruction, warning or command followed by a punishment. Three gave an instruction, but followed it by a warning about the conse-quences or a repetition of the instruction. However, one was consistent in offering the hypothetical child choices of alter-native settings in which to carry out an activity. *Offering choices* in this way is a principle upheld by parenting programmes.

Roger: 'If you were Jo's mummy, what would you say? What would be the good thing to say?'

CSB: 'If you want to jump on something, you can jump on the bouncy castle.'

Roger: 'Let's just pretend that Jo carries on jumping on the sofa. If you were Jo's mummy, what would you say then?' [silence]

Roger: [Returning to the question later] 'now one of the questions was what would you do if Jo carries on jumping on the sofa. What would you say then? What would you say?'

CSB: 'Do you want to go on a trampoline?'

Roger: 'And how would that make Jo feel?'

CSB: 'Happier.'

The responses indicated a fascinating variation among children's perceptions of how to resolve parenting difficulties.

Siblings dispute

Disputes between siblings are a common topic of parenting education (Hartley-Brewer, 1996). Would the children see the situation as simply disorderly, or would they encourage 'fair play'?

One child took over control of the situation and denied both siblings their wishes; another considered this possibility. A third instructed the two to stop arguing.

The rest insisted on some form of turn-taking, for example, by chance ('heads or tails') or a 'first-come-first-served' principle. In some responses the principle of fairness was unclear. Two clearly gave priority to the main character of the story, while a third favoured the second sibling.

Most of the children saw parents as arbiters who would draw on some principle of fairness in order to settle disputes, even though this was not always clear.

Untidiness

Keeping a bedroom or play space in order is a standard topic for communication strategies in parenting programmes (see Parent Network (1988) References section, *Labels*, p 3).

Responding to untidiness was straightforward for most of the children. Nine gave an instruction to tidy up, typically avoiding a negative message (such as 'don't make a mess'), while just one made a request. Three talked about possible punishments. Two referred to the *logical consequences* of untidiness (Quinn and Quinn, 1995).

> CKM: 'No. If they spoil their clothes they won't get no more and they'll have to be naked.'
>
> CTEL: 'I'd say to him, "Joe, go and tidy up your clothes," and if he like didn't do it, or didn't do it that day then, couple of days later, he's started, not doing it again, I'd say, "We are just going to leave it like that, see if your clothes are going to build up and build up, then you won't have no clean clothes to wear out."'

Respectful approaches like these, which would attract the approval of parent education providers, emerged in a minority of cases.

Praise and criticism

Children were asked to respond to mistakes made by a hypothetical child trying to help the parent. This scenario contained possibilities for both praise and criticism. A number of responses took a positive line, though none ignored the mistakes (Table 7.3). Despite the one clearly negative response, children in the sample described various ways of handling the situation respectfully.

Table 7.3   Responses

Instruction to correct mistakes	3
Helping or teaching	3
Thanks or praise	2
Inquire and correct	1
Inform child of error	1
Label and banish	1

Contact with close relative living far away

Contact with relatives is a significant issue for 'transnational' families and others whose members are separated (Moore, Sixsmith and Knowles, 1996). Children in the sample mentioned several practical measures to maintain contact (Table 7.4).

Table 7.4   Responses

Visits	5
Telephone contact	2
Locate relative	1
Holiday with relative	1
Information and encouragement	1
Tell child about relative's unavailability	1

According to the twelve-year-old a parent would seek to build in the child's mind an image of the relative.

CTEL: 'I would tell him like, "One day, when you're a bit older we can go and see your grandma", and I'd describe her to him tell him what she's like, her personality, some things about her.'

Roger: 'And how'd that make him feel?'

CTEL: 'I think it would make him understand that if he doesn't know someone, ask someone about them, so he could find out about them.'

Encouragement – school testing

Because parents' attitudes to educational performance have increased in social significance, responses to preparations for school testing and examination were explored. How far would the children be realistic and encouraging towards the hypothetical child?

Five of the children declined to respond or did not know what a test was. Most tried to press home the significance of the test or to give encouragement and praise; only one communicated a negative message, (Table 7.5).

Table 7.5   Responses

Reaffirm goal	2
Encourage	2
Praise	1
Help	1
Negative message and warning	1

Resolving ambiguities

A number of children saw unusual complaints about headaches as a medical matter, while others were suspicious or downright dismissive, (Table 7.6).

Table 7.6   Responses

Obtain medical assistance	3
Check symptom	2
Bed rest	1
Offer medicine	1
Dismiss symptom	1
Check symptom but express suspicion and warn	2
Encourage to continue, feeling suspicious	1

The suspicious responses are particularly interesting because they involve acting with two different hypotheses in mind. In the oldest child, suspicions were not expressed but withheld.

> CTEL: 'I would say like, "Go to school, try and get on with it, if you don't feel very well, tell the teacher, teacher would phone me and you'll be able to come home and have a rest in bed and if you don't feel well later on, we'll phone the doctor".'
>
> 'I think the one where you had a headache, you said it one week and you said it the next week, and then the week after, or it might be on the same specific day because he does not like the subject he's got, he's trying to skive that day. That's how I found it.'

Understanding this difference between surface intention and what lies beneath it is identified as a higher developmental achievement by Selman (1980).

Conclusion

In order to put these findings in a broader context, it is worthwhile comparing them with the results of a recent survey of children aged from eight to fifteen years (Ghate and Daniels, 1997). Personal regard and care (kindness, listening, spending time with children) and modelling good behaviour (example-setting, keeping promises) emerged as major qualities of 'good parents'. Strictness was not viewed as a major quality, nor was providing material things. It follows that parenting programmes which handle relationship issues as well as misbehaviour are consistent with children's agenda.

Another relevant finding of the survey was that, according to children, parents of all cultural backgrounds seemed to have a fairly uniform approach to strictness with their children.

In that study, children seemed to endorse their own parents' style of parenting, indicating a significant continuity between generations. The foundations of tomorrow's parenting are being laid today.

Of course, children in the present study were not specifically asked to rate the qualities of good parents. But they did approach the concrete task of choosing tactics of communication which were meant to be expressions of a good parent's sense of responsibility. It is clear from the present study that children do have an appreciation of the responsibilities of parenthood. They are also attuned to the variety of situations to which parents are expected to respond. They envisaged parents as arbiters, setting limits, and correcting disobedience. The differences in response to the same hypothetical situations indicate the range of responses they can envisage, even at similar ages. Some of these responses correspond to the 'good enough parent' portrayed in parenting programmes, while a number do not. It is however, fascinating to observe cases where tactics chosen by children do agree with 'expert' opinion. All the children – and not just these precocious experts – appear to be learning to be parents.

8 What should programmes seek to achieve?

Parents and agents alike were asked to define desirable outcomes. The evidence indicates how far the two groups shared common ground.

Parents' views about outcomes

All parents interviewed, whether they had experience of programmes or not, were invited to say what they expected to get out of a programme. Their responses were then categorised (Table 8.1). The most frequently mentioned were group outcomes, such as comparing individual experiences with other people's. These were followed, in order of frequency, by a better relationship with the children, greater knowledge, and emotional benefits.

Asked to state the *most* important, parents spread their choices across these categories or chose more than one. Relationship outcomes were rarely specified on their own as a primary outcome.

Parents were then asked to envisage important outcomes for their children. Rather than seeing the programmes as a foundation for achieving particular goals, parents envisaged more direct influences on the mutual relationship of parents and children. The most frequent replies, from about half the respondents, mentioned improvements in the parent–child relationship, such as behaviour changes and understanding. Almost three out of ten referred to a child's emotions, such as happiness or greater confidence. Only one in ten mentioned particular aspects of a child's needs, such as being healthy, making educational progress or meeting special needs.

If outcomes are to extend in to the future, how should the immediate impact be defined and related to future tasks and challenges? Parents were invited to distinguish 'short term'

Table 8.1 Outcomes envisaged by parents

Group outcomes	**43 references by 31 respondents**
Networks	
Friends	
Compare self with others	
Learn from other parents	
Relationship outcomes	**38 references by 27 respondents**
Understanding child	
Communication	
Relationship	
Resolve problem	
Less conflict	
Knowledge outcomes	**30 references by 25 respondents**
Health outcomes	
Development	
Education	
Emotional outcomes	**26 references by 20 respondents**
Less anxiety	
Raise confidence	
Happiness	
Less stress	

from 'long term' benefits. The short term meant any benefit occurring immediately or in the months following a programme. The long term was defined as a period extending beyond a year after the course.

Many of the responses concerning the short term were repetitions of previously stated outcomes; a small proportion were more focused on equipping the parent for the future. Equipping the parents for the future was much more recognisable among the attenders' responses (Table 8.2).

As for the remainder, several mentioned combinations of outcomes that had already been raised. There were a handful of individual responses identifying particular benefits, such as getting some recognition for having attended a course or having something to fall back on if needed. One denied that short-term outcomes were important, and another could not foresee any. The rest were unsure or did not offer any thoughts.

Table 8.2   Short-term benefits

Progress to goal	
Outcome as stated previously	15
Improvement in relationship	3
Equipping parent	
Knowledge or skill	7
Practice	3
Partners sharing common approach	3

The long term (Table 8.3) was conceived by some as an extension of the process of achieving outcomes, rather than as a qualitatively new phase. A minority saw the implications stretching up to a child's maturity. There were several responses identifying combinations of benefits or various individual wishes. A few denied the relevance of the long term. The remainder were unsure or did not provide any views.

Table 8.3   Long-term benefits

Outcome as previously stated	15
Benefits when the child matures	8
Keeping up good parenting	6

Attenders again were more likely to acknowledge the need to 'keep it up', not to lose ground. Like the others, however, it appeared that they sensed the future as an open extension of the present. Their sense of the future as relatively unspecific is understandable. Unlike professionals, parents have before them few well defined benchmarks, like curricular targets.

This is not to say that once having accessed a programme parents envisaged that all would be plain sailing. Some suggested that they should be contacted at a later date as a form of auditing progress. In fact, virtually half the sample said that they would find a follow up course useful. And an eighth thought they possibly might take up that option.

'having them there later on maybe that you can go back to [the facilitators], yeah. If you have any other problems or maybe finding out a different course if there is one that they can do or there is one they know of. Yeah, being there again for later on down the line.' (209)

Agents' views about outcomes

In order to compare the outcomes envisaged by the different stakeholders, similar open ended questions were put to agents. In Table 8.4, to simplify the comparison, the broad responses about outcomes were aggregated with responses on the specific outcomes for the short and long term.

Table 8.4   Outcomes envisaged by agents

For parents	Indications
Emotions such as happiness and confidence	14
Group support	9
Relationship with child	7
Knowledge or understanding	5
Personal empowerment	5
For child	
Children's emotions	3
Child behaviour	1
Child identity	1
Child social skills	1
Educational progress	2

The consensus of the agents, from various backgrounds, bears interesting resemblances to the views of parents. There was a clear recognition of emotional benefits for parents and for children. This emphasis was particularly evident among facilitators. The supportive functions of the groups were acknowledged.

'Parents themselves, I would like to think were more confident, that they are more relaxed and less stressed and that in itself must have a spin off as to how they relate with their children . . . I think the really telling part would be kind of six months down the line, whether they felt that they could, they had sort of kept up some of the resolves and promises they've made to themselves at that time. I think that if the parents actually keep in contact with the programme remain as a support to each other there is more likelihood of that happening.' (104)

There was also some understanding that parents should be given the power to fashion their own destinies rather than be spoon-fed an approved diet. Such appreciation chimes well with parents' own statements: in the last analysis they were to make the decisions and take the consequences.

The evidence suggests that these agents shared a broad agenda with parents about the desirable outcomes of parenting programmes.

9 Towards a shared framework for assessment

In concluding this report it makes sense to start from principles of programme assessment rather than to be preoccupied at this stage with methods. This discussion begins with the core implications of the findings, focusing on the issues for parents and children before examining the policy and strategic questions that should be addressed.

If parenting education and support is to be organised on a shared footing then any framework for assessment must acknowledge the importance of these seven key themes:

Allowing parents to share experiences
Inclusive approaches
Equal accessibility
Knowledge as empowerment
Children as stakeholders
Clear evidence-based policies
Strategic coherence from top to bottom.

Sharing the experience of parenting

It is striking how parenting has moved into public discourse yet there has not been a comparable development of ways for parents to share their experiences in a non-judgemental setting. Parents interviewed in this study had a strong commitment to parenting as a continuous and demanding set of responsibilities – feelings that can lead to guilt and anxiety. Such parents do not seem to need lessons in parental responsibility. Indeed one significant purpose of parenting programmes is to encourage them to find ways of looking after themselves. Parents wanted some increase in confidence that stems from having compared their experiences with others. They saw the development and maintenance of networks as a logical continuation of this mutual sharing – even if this simply means watching a regular parenting show on television, as one parent suggested.

An inclusive approach

It is clear that the outcomes envisaged by parents and agents were similar. It is interesting to consider some reasons why this may have been so. Agents, of course, have been trained to work with families. Typically, the facilitators had attended programmes as participants. Nevertheless, it seems that agents viewed open access programmes partly through the prism of their own experience of parenting, especially as mothers. Using group support to assuage anxiety makes good sense to professionals who may have had similar experiences. They can intuitively understand the benefits to mothers which can arise from the groups. The strength of parenting programmes lies in this understanding. However there are limitations in an approach which builds on past experience and fails to take on the challenge of including parents whose roles are categorised in different ways, for example the role of father.

Compared with the needs of mothers, fathers' needs did not seem to be so intuitively appreciated by professionals. Only one of the groups had recruited a man and this pattern is known to be typical. It is possible to understand why the needs of fathers do not have the same prominence. Because fathers are not perceived as significant providers of direct care they are not given the same attention. Yet it can be argued that this perception is neither realistic nor helpful towards the long-term well-being of children (Burgess and Ruxton, 1996).

The experiences of parents who felt isolated in their groups tell a similar story. If parents can not recognise someone in the group with whom they can identify, they are unlikely to find the group experience very comfortable. Groups should be balanced, or, if necessary, set up for particular groups of parents.

It is important to acknowledge the principle of inclusiveness without assuming that every group should be representative. For example, some women, as well as men, may be distinctly uncomfortable in a mixed group.

Accessibility

There is a good case for making equal accessibility into a major principle guiding 'open access' services (Sinclair, Hearn and Pugh, 1997). The public profile of programmes is very low, meaning that many parents will be unaware of any services that exist. Public information strategies can make a contribution to raising and clarifying awareness. Practical problems of access were frequently experienced by parents in the sample. Resources are therefore needed to back up wider participation. In some cases it may be appropriate to rethink the service in order to foster and sustain participation. For example, the development of video-based education presents a way of engaging people who may find group discussion inaccessible.

Knowledge as empowerment

Parents did not regard the content of a programme or its knowledge base as critical (Barber, 1992). It is hard to identify any alternative agenda which parents counter-posed to the content of the programmes. It was a means to an end. Yet this does not imply that content was irrelevant. The content had to be *empowering*. It should be instrumental in enabling parents to make clear and positive choices by giving them 'tips' or 'ideas'. The presentation should not patronise parents by speaking down to them or make them feel powerless by laying down the law. Instead it must generate an atmosphere of acceptance and optimism through which parents can be receptive to new ideas. Once these are tried out with any success, belief in the value of the suggestions is reinforced.

One of the implications of the findings is that parents are open to new ideas and are prepared to implement them if they feel that other parents have worked successfully with them.

In looking at long-term outcomes, it seems reasonable to conclude that parents will be more inclined to persist if they have absorbed the idea that the 'tips' can contribute to a long-term strategy by which they reflect on their experiences and adjust them as the child grows. Follow up by some form of auditing or going on new courses was a widely endorsed way of handling the uncertainties of the future.

Children as stakeholders

Children are not raw material for parents to operate with; they develop a sense of the responsibilities and communicative styles of parenthood. If, as seems likely, such learning is a formative process for the next generation of parents, then it is essential that children's views must enter the debate on parenting education and support.

The messages from this research can influence the content of programmes by encouraging them to alert parents to children's views. Parenting courses advocate the importance of listening to children and establishing a basis for respectful communication. Materials that directly give a voice to children, even anonymously, can be a valuable confirmation of the child-centred approach which the textbooks recommend.

Clear evidence-based policies

It is possible to identify two key themes in arguments for services of this kind: a major theme is concerned with first line prevention; the other is a promotional theme, about raising standards.

Health and education each present examples of these themes in action. Health targets can be set to avert negative health outcomes, reducing the need for interventions, but it is feasible also to formulate a policy that actively seeks to cultivate conditions for the health and growth of all. In principle, there are no upper limits to the outcomes that might be envisaged. In many ways, education is seen in these positive terms, as a service that can be the foundation for higher and higher goals.

Arguments for preventive services must be based on good evidence. In order to be preventive, it is necessary that the coverage be very wide, that a procedure, whether parenting education or immunisation, is effective, that it should be associated with a measurable reduction of problems in the population and it should be reasonably cost effective. These are tough requirements and not easy to satisfy, particularly over the long term. Various complex methodologies have been proposed to ascertain whether particular services have the effects intended (Oakley and Roberts, 1996).

Nevertheless one of the first tasks is how to ensure take-up on the scale necessary to demonstrate the effects. In principle a major challenge for primary prevention is to persuade enough people with few or no current problems that they are at sufficient risk to make it worthwhile using a service. Moreover, they have to be able to grasp how any benefits from the service now will arm them to face future difficulties. This risk and benefit assessment is especially difficult in the field of parenting because a child's future cannot be readily predicted. It may be very easy to sell the service to some of the 'worried well' who are unlikely to face significant problems. But what about the rest?

However, these challenges do not seem so great if it is possible to convince people that there are also short-term benefits from a service that are more easily graspable. In the case of parenting programmes, parents seem to envisage immediate benefits that they hope will extend into the future. Research on prevention will have to encompass not only the assessment of risk, but also short- and long-term benefits, if it is to underpin a realistic preventive policy.

There are more urgent and persuasive public interest arguments for preventive services than for promotional ones. There would be few objections to policies that relieved parental stress or offered new ways of handling family problems if it could be shown that they were likely to avert damaging conflict or disruption. Promoting new standards of parenting is more debatable, even controversial. How would it be possible to choose among the promotional goals on offer, especially if they were contradictory? However there is a line of argument which would suggest that empowering parents with information about alternatives is a public good in itself. This would leave it to parents to make the choice, rather like choosing a language for study. The merits of any proposal to encourage particular adjustments in family experiences or relationships would be the subject of excited debate but one which encouraged the provision of learning opportunities and information might attract support from a spectrum of interested parties.

Public policy might then seek ways of actively fostering proven preventive strategies and services (thus with the highest ranking) and also encouraging a diversity of alternative provision (ranking second).

Strategies

Strategies are essential building blocks for the development of services. It will be interesting to see what happens when the agencies involved in this research have to engage with broad policy or strategic shifts in the future. Will their parenting initiatives be strengthened or weakened? If professionals want this kind of initiative to prosper then they will be well advised to formulate an explicit framework of aims and objectives for undertaking this work, backed by a strategy for implementation. Strategic thinking means bringing agencies together to agree a common plan of action. However, there seems to have been no systematic evidence-based exploration of local models of strategic planning that agencies can usefully draw upon.

The organisational character of programmes as **limited projects** poses considerable problems in sustaining or increasing their accessibility to a wide population.

- Interagency coordination is dependent on exceptional initiatives like the one supporting P3.
- There is a big information gap which means that recruitment is very personalised and can be interrupted by any number of factors.
- Small localities close to a venue are targeted without any broader assessment of need.
- There are no incentives to recruit any more cases than can be handled by the practitioners available.
- Small numbers also mean that scope for conclusive local evaluation is limited.
- Funding is vulnerable to strategic cost cutting.
- Major commissioners may have little specific awareness about small programmes which are maintained on sufferance because they do not fit rigid funding formulas.

As the experience of P2 illustrates, multiagency approaches are not necessarily part of a strategy; they can be opportunistic developments which are intended to overcome administrative problems and facilitate access to resources.

All this means that there is no guarantee that the progress identified by the research will continue. The convergence of views found in this research stems partly from the dominance of practitioners in setting the goals of programmes. A number have participated in programmes themselves. They know from experience how it feels to take part and what works in the field. Managers and other agents are then often themselves converted and recruited to the cause of carrying out the programmes.

It must be asked whether this is sustainable if programmes are to be generalised across organisations and areas. Will commissioners, distant from the field, seek to become dominant and set new possibly conflicting goals? In order to maintain the integrity of programme goals it is important to keep information flowing upwards as well as downwards and across. There needs to be a *strategic plan* and an *active executive body* to identify and spread good practice, along the lines developing in the county where P3 was based. Yet there should be the possibility of active *representations* upwards too.

In some respects the case of P3 points up the positive possibilities for the future. The idea of a strategic forum as pioneered in P3 is a significant step forward. It helped to foster an alliance of understanding between a senior practitioner (the head teacher) and the representative of a large multidisciplinary forum stretching across the county. Instead of leading the initiative, the facilitator was chosen after the plan for the project had been formulated. Strategy was therefore the determining factor, rather than practitioner preferences. At the same time there was a positive consensus about the aims of the service. If progress is to be made at a national level, information about any similar strategic models should be collected and shared.

Appendix: Child interview guide

If . . .

If something happens, what should parents say? **You decide
. . .!** *(Version for girls)*

*Jo likes to play by jumping off and on the pavement. She is
going to the shops with her friend, and the road will be very
busy with traffic.*

If you were her mother, what would you say?

*Jo is playing at home with her Lego bricks. She wants to build
a bridge. She is looking at the bricks and trying to fit some
together. Her mother has finished the washing up and comes
into the room. She sits down on the sofa.*

If you were her mother, what would you say?

*Jo has done something her mother says she should not do. Can
you imagine something like that? What do you imagine she
has done?*

If you were Jo's mother, what would you say?

Jo carries on doing the same thing.

If you were Jo's mother, what would you say?

*Jo and her sister would like to watch different videos on the
television. Her sister sits down and says, 'It's my turn'. Jo says
to her mother 'It's my turn'.*

If you were Jo's mother, what would you say?

*Jo is expected to keep her things tidy in her bedroom. Jo's
mother finds clothes scattered on the floor of the bedroom. This
happens a lot, thinks Jo's mum.*

If you were Jo's mother, what would you say?

After a big dinner Jo has helped her mother with a lot of washing up and put away the dishes. Some of the dishes are in the wrong places.

If you were Jo's mother, what would you say?

Jo has a granny who lives in a country far away. Do you have anyone in your family who lives a long way from you? Well Jo lives hundreds of miles away from her granny. It's a whole year since Jo saw her granny. Jo's mum knows where granny is.

If you were Jo's mum, what would you say to Jo about her granny?

Jo's had a test in school. It's about maths. That's counting and sums. The teacher has sent the results to Jo's mum. Jo says, 'I'm just no good at these tests. When the proper exam comes round, maybe it'll be different. Anyway, loads of other kids think maths is boring.'

If you were Jo's mum, what would be a good thing to say to Jo?

Jo tells her Mum she has a headache. Do you know what that is?

'Not another one!' says Mum. 'You had one last week and the week before. You are usually so well.'

If you were Jo's mum, what would be a good thing to say to Jo?

(The version for boys contained the main character 'Joe'.)

References

Allan, J (1994) 'Parenting education in Australia', *Children & Society*, 8, 4, 344–59

Barber, J (1992) 'Evaluating Parent Education Groups: effects on sense of competence and social isolation', *Research on Social Work Practice*, 2, 1, 28–38

Barlow, J (1997) *Systematic Review of the Effectiveness of Parent-Training Programmes in improving behaviour problems in children aged 3–10 years. A review of the literature on parent-training programmes and child behaviour outcome measures.* Health Services Research Unit, Department of Public Health, Oxford

Brannen, J and O'Brien, M eds (1996) *Children in families: research and policy.* Falmer Press

Burgess, A and Ruxton, S (1996) *Men and their children: Proposals for public policy.* Institute for Public Policy Research

Centre for Educational Research and Innovation (CERI) (1997) *Parents as Partners in Schooling.* Organisation for Economic Co-operation and Development

Collins, M (1997) 'Cycle safety among infant school children', *Health Education*, 1, 30–34

Davis, H and Hester, P (1997) *An independent evaluation of Parent-Link, a parenting education programme developed by Parent Network.* Academic Unit of Child and Adolescent Psychiatry and Psychology, United Medical and Dental School

Dembo, M, Sweitzer, M and Lauritzen, P (1985) 'An evaluation of Group Parent Education: Behavioural, PET and Adlerian Programmes', *Review of Educational Research*, 55, 2, 155–200

Doherty, W and Ryder, R (1980) 'Parent Effectiveness Training (P.E.T.): criticisms and caveats', *Journal of Marital and Family Therapy*, X, 409–419

Fine, M ed. (1989) *The second handbook on parent education.* New York: Academic Press

Ghate, D and Daniels, A (1997) *Talking about my generation.* National Society for the Prevention of Cruelty to Children

Guba, E G and Lincoln, Y S (1989) *Fourth generation evaluation.* Sage Publications

Hartley-Brewer, E (1994) *Positive Parenting: Raising children with self-esteem.* CEDAR

Hartley-Brewer, E (1996) *Cooperative Kids.* Facilitator's Resource Pack

Hess, R (1980) 'Experts and amateurs: some unintended consequences of parent education' *in* Fantini, M and Cardenas, R *eds Parenting in Multicultural Society.* Longman

L'Abate, L (1990) *Building family competence: Primary and secondary prevention strategies.* Sage Publications

Malek, M (1996) 'Home–school work'. *Highlight 145.* National Children's Bureau

Medway, F (1989) 'Measuring the effectiveness of parent education' Chapter 10 *in* Fine, M *ed. The second handbook of parent education.* New York: Academic Press

Moore, M, Sixsmith, J and Knowles, K (1996) *Children's Reflections on Family Life.* Falmer Press

Nicholas, D and Marden, M (1997) *The Information Needs of Parents. Case Study: parents of children under the age of five.* British Library Research and Innovation Report 56. The British Library

O'Brien, M, Alldred, P and Jones, D (1996) 'Children's constructions of family and kinship' *in* Brannen, J and O'Brien, M *eds Children in families: research and policy.* Falmer Press

Oakley, A and Roberts, H (1996) *Evaluating social interventions: a report of two workshops funded by the Economic and Social Research Council.* Social Science Research Unit/Barnardos

Parent Network (1988) Coordinator guide for Parent-link Part One. Twelve two-and-a-half hour sessions. Folder and 12 booklets

Parr, M (1996) *Support for couples in the transition to parenthood.* Unpublished Ph.D thesis. Department of Psychology, University of East London

Patterson, G R, Chamberlain, P and Reid, J B (1982) 'A comparative evaluation of a parent-training program', *Behaviour Therapy*, 13, 5, 638–50

Pugh, G (1994) *Effective Parenting Programmes for Schools: A Pilot Study.* Unpublished paper

Pugh, G, De'Ath, E and Smith, C (1994) *Confident Parents, Confident Children Policy and Practice in Parent Education and Support.* National Children's Bureau

Quinn, M and Quinn, T (1995) *From Pram to Primary School: Parenting small children from birth to age six or seven.* Family Caring Trust

Roberts, C and others (1995) *A national study of parents and parenting problems. Working Paper 1.* Family Policy Studies Centre

Roker, D and Coleman, J (1998) *Parenting Programmes: A UK Perspective.* A report on research funded by The Gulbenkian Foundation

Selman, R (1980) *The growth of interpersonal understanding. Developmental and clinical analyses.* London, New York: Academic Press

Sinclair, R, Hearn, B and Pugh, G (1997) *The contribution of mainstream services to preventive work with families.* A discussion paper for the Joseph Rowntree Foundation

Smith, C (1996) *Developing Parenting Programmes.* National Children's Bureau

Straw, J and Anderson, J (1996) *Parenting. A discussion paper.* Labour Party

Tamivaara, J and Enright, D S (1986) 'On eliciting information: dialogues with child informants', *Anthropology and Education Quarterly*, 17, 218–38

Ulich, M and Oberhuermer, P (1993) 'Images of the family: on interviewing young children about their social concepts', *Early Years Education*, 1, 1, 13–21

Utting, D (1995) 'Family and parenthood: supporting families, preventing breakdown', *Childright,* 116, 5/6, 17–18

Webster-Stratton, C (1984) 'Randomised trial of two parent-training programs for families with conduct-disorder children', *Journal of Clinical Psychology*, 52, 4, 666–78

Williams, T, Wetton, N and Moon, A (1989) *Health for Life 1: A Teacher's Planning Guide to Health Education in the Primary School*. Health Education Authority/Nelson

Yin, R (1989) *Case study research. Design and methods* (rev. edn). Sage

Index